the silence
between
what i think
and
what i say

stephan silich

BROOKLYN
WRITERS PRESS

the silence between what i think and what i say copyright © 2018 by Stephan Silich. All rights reserved. Printed in the United States of America. No part of this book may be used or reproduced in any manner whatsoever without written permission except in the case of brief quotations embodied in critical articles and reviews.

Brooklyn Writers Press
Brooklyn, NY
www.brooklynwriterspress.com

ISBN 978-0-9997903-1-1

LCCN 2018957190

Cover photo by Stephan Silich
Jacket design by Marina Aris

for my daughters, emma and mia,
you have unquestionably given meaning to my life i had absolutely
no right to ever expect.
even words fail, when i try to express how much i love you both.

for my brother, robert,
you are the emblem of fortitude and inexplicable strength.
you are the only person i know who is always a gentleman.

for my mother, dianne, and father, robert
you gave me the greatest gift of all,
a childhood full of love and laughter,
and later the courage and inspiration
to create my own family.

this is for all of you.

it was always for all of you.

thank you.

"I will hold your heart more tenderly than my own."

- Bench Plaque, Central Park, New York

contents

foreword	11
one	13
the girl	15
risk everything	16
rejoice	17
somewhere on 2nd avenue	18
desolate angels	20
what i'll do	21
the deep-cleansing facial	22
dinner at renatos	24
still	25
overlooking the blue pool	26
the shivering ends of my fingers	27
what counts	28
for you	29
possibility	30
centuries	31
the fragile elements	32
for alan	33
blood and effort	37
life lived right	39
let us re-enact our exhausted love	41
everything will surrender to time, except...	42
art & love	43
the answers to the secrets	45
two	47
a glimpse of a disappearing way of life	49
when i die	51
only ever, looking forward	52
don't you know	53
i also believe...	54
ode to new york	55
the sweetest thing	62

new york 2012	63
across time and space	64
native son	65
for emma	67
some advice to get you through	70
the little pleasures worth dying for	74
what will you be thinking in the final moments?	76
remember	77
i am waiting	79
three	**83**
open the window please	85
the little ones	86
testament	87
begin	89
the art of dying	91
for mia	93
the arrival	96
life	98
school	100
easter with emma	102
the art of unsung work	103
look past them	105
kindness	107
for pop	109
four	**113**
the smile	115
celebrate	116
the blind side of your soul	117
out the front door	118
no heat	119
the wordless portrait	120
you will find it right there	123
as i write from bed on a monday night	126
today	127
through my soul	128
keep going	130
my lost summer	131
a note from my mom	134
my victory	135

window seat 15a	137
the glamorous outlaw	138
in the midst of life	140
an old man's life	141

five   143

the secret	145
i am still	147
no one will know	148
all i remember	149
a life without vulgarity	150
under the low winter sun	151
one-room apartment	152
for my brother	154
outside the morgan library on 36th and madison	155
lying on a tar roof above the city	157
anonymous	158
for the girl	159
good neighbors	161
endurance	166
warmed by wine	167
the beautiful ones	168
miracles	169
fight	170
brief self-interview	172
in these hours	173
for emma & mia	175
the silence between what i think and what i say	176

acknowledgements	181
about the author	183

foreword

"All art should be free." This is what Stephan said to me so many years ago when I asked if he would ever publish his work. He seemed satisfied with gifting hand-bound collections to close friends and family. I never thought the day would come when he would agree to have his work published. Fortunately for me, his publisher, and for you, the reader holding this book in your hands, the day has come, it only took nearly two decades to get here.

Time has many faces, and for most of us it is all too fleeting, but there are moments like these, when time brings forth something meaningful enough to quell the human spirit. Something to slow down the pace and remind you to pay attention. Something to encourage you to love and lose a little bit more, because in the end it is all worth it. This collection is the product of time. And in the countless silent hours that have come to pass, Stephan has crafted an extensive body of work. Work that I feel honored and privileged to publish.

In these pages, what will make its way through the silence is Stephan's voice. A voice that is at once fresh and familiar. Tender and thoughtful. Endearing and haunting. Words that will carry you back to the innocence of childhood, to the fragile yearnings of love, and then gently guide you forward to the preoccupations of adulthood and parenthood. And finally they will lift your spirit after placing you mindfully into the center of your own mortality.

Stephan is a devoted father now, and although I'd like to believe that only time has changed his perspective on publishing his work, it is the love for his daughters, Emma and Mia, that are the true motivation for allowing this work to be published. I imagine them years into the future finding hope and love and comfort in their father's words. What better gift can a father leave for his children?

Stephan did once firmly believe that art should be free. But as a writer and publisher I hold a different belief. And that is, that art should be freed. And it is in that spirit that I offer you dear reader this collection. May it fill your silent hours with hope and love and comfort.

Marina Aris
Publisher, Brooklyn Writers Press
December, 2018

I.

for the hearts
that beat loudest
during the quietest of moments . . .

the girl

it's an encounter that
leaves you with an indelible image
that is both impossible to forget
yet complete agony to behold.

she compels your absolute attention
and elicits that rarified ache that
never seems to go away.

she is an unexpected expectation.

she is your sense of time and place,
importance and relevance,
moving through you
and through these moments
straight to the remembrance
of all things,
past and present.

risk everything

it is the only way
to find the answers
to the all-important questions
of what you want in life,
and what you may or may not
settle for.

accept the irresistible possibility
of what you can't ignore,
wrap your arms around the meaning
of every soul
and the breathless mystery
of every existence.

rejoice

remember
when you find it,
when you really find it,
it is your obligation
to stay together,
relentlessly,
until
the very last minute of life.

and so, until then,
i will rejoice in the small events
marking the passage of time:

the sound of my mother's slippers
across the kitchen floor,
the first bite of the cheeseburger,
the last sip of wine,
the quiet calm after a long cry,
the feel of my bare feet on the sand,
the laziness of sunday,

and us sleeping
in the afternoon sun
with great stillness,
making time dissolve,
and rendering the sun
and moon
equally irrelevant.

somewhere on 2nd avenue

the nurse
placed her warm hands
on my neck
and then down my back
looking for any abnormalities
while i coughed,
turned,
breathed in
breathed out.

i closed my eyes
and took in
this sense of touch.

when you're alone
you take what you can get.

later that night,
i saw my ex-girlfriend
walking down 2nd avenue
and i just sat there and watched her
with that walk i still remember so well.

and there is still a part of me
that would like to run up those five flights of stairs
and lie next to her
on the white couch under the open window
where we slept on cold nights,
welcoming the night noise
that always kept us up for hours.

but it was ok
because those
long unslept hours

gave us more time
to take in those new york moments,
which once were beautiful
but now
only break my heart
over
and
over
and
over
again.

desolate angels

the victimized
the poor
the unemployed
the misfits
the abused
the working class
the skid row bums
the drunk poets
the dispossessed painters
the outlaws
the betrayed
the brutalized
the beaten
and the mad.

your lives unfold
almost matter-of-factly,
and you continue
to go unnoticed and uncared for,
yet you'll manage to give us
touches of melancholy beauty.

yours will be a heartbreaking finish,
i can assure you,
and they will point
their manicured fingers at you,
declaring you a failure.

but remember,
it may appear that you've failed at
everything you did,
but you will never fail
at the most important thing of all,
which is life.

what i'll do

although sorrow occasionally
gains momentum
on this bleached language of truth

i still believe in the poetic
and offbeat charm
of living on the far edges of life,
where the pace is slower,
and where most professional aspirations
are eschewed for a simple and quiet contentment.

i've always found immense charm
in seeing lives lived differently from the rest,
and i've always embraced
this too intimate understanding
of the way the world should work.

i witness these honest moments of clarity
and push past the ache i see in every face.

i'll ask the gods
to guide me with compassion and decency.

i'll embrace the nights of contemplation
that turn into mornings of solace,
and i'll keep believing despite the losses.

the deep-cleansing facial

booked a 50 minute treatment,
which i do once every couple of years.

took the italian scooter over,
checked in,
grabbed a robe
and headed to the room.

our conversation was easy and polite
until she mentioned she had lost her soulmate.

he died at 57 of an aortic aneurysm which, she explained, meant his heart valve burst and blood filled his lungs and that was it.

i asked when he died, and she said about five years ago.
i told her i may have lost my soulmate also about two years ago,
but there was
no death,
only a betrayal,
and luckily
my heart valve didn't burst – at least not yet.

she said sometimes, when the person is still around, it's even harder, but i wasn't so sure.

she said she believed the soul has a certain amount of time with another and that it may be a year or it may be a lifetime, but what makes it beautiful is that we never know when that time comes to an end.

we stayed quiet until she spoke of her childhood home on the mediterranean coast where her mom taught her it was ok to touch the earth, talk to the flowers, and stare at the stars.

then more silence.

as my facial neared its end,
she placed my hands in warm, heated gloves and
then moisturized and massaged from my elbows to my fingertips.
as she held my hand in hers,
i couldn't help but notice how small and delicate they were,
but in that smallness, i could feel a world of hope and goodness.

i think she held my hand for a little longer than is usual
for a standard facial,
but that was more than ok,
because underneath the ridiculous frozen cucumbers over my eyes,
one petulant tear started to make its way down my cheek,
and she gently wiped it away without ever acknowledging it.

and that was the end of my deep-cleansing facial.

dinner at renatos
(april 30th, 2009)

with my parents and brother
celebrating my birthday.

my brother lifted his glass and said:

"here's to you on your 40th -
the kindest person i know."

it was the nicest compliment
i could ever hope for.

and on that breeze-filled,
75-degree night
under the palms
and hanging wisteria,
we ordered another bottle of wine,
because we all knew
this was our night to burn.

still

in that new york bookstore,
on that new york night,
a few smiles exchanged,
a few words shared,
and a long walk
through the streets of greenwich village,
ending at washington square park
at the foot of 5th avenue
alongside the central fountain.

it was a welcomed interruption
on an ordinary night.

and i'm dreaming now
with my eyes open
because there's still a bit of your face
i haven't kissed.

there's still many of your words
i haven't heard.

there's still the touch of your hand
i want in my hand.

there's still the future of your tears
i promise to wipe away.

and there's still your beauty
that lights the candle
and burns through the night,
illuminating all that you are to me.

overlooking the blue pool

the crumbling stones
and the discolored bricks
and the stained marble
and the scratched porcelain
and the peeling paint
and the cracked floor
and the chipped mirror

all shadows of another way of life.

and the face of this land
is brilliant again
under the summer sun.

wine is being made,
music is being listened to
and youth and beauty
give love a chance
in the upstairs bedroom
overlooking the blue pool.

the shivering ends of my fingers

the unpredictable lushness of emotion,

the desperate urgency of limitless possibility,

the wilderness of discordant feelings,

the midlife upheaval of the human spirit,

the creative illness of infinite despondence,

the descent into exhilarating and hopeful madness,

the unspoken questions on this unshadowed earth,

the emphasis on privacy and understatement,

the unmistakable privilege of your nudity,

and the pleasures of incompleteness

while the shivering ends of my fingers

continue to write these words

for the hearts that beat loudest

during the quietest of moments.

what counts

the discerning accuracy of silence.

the contentment of the fragile recovery.

the dignity of being loyal
to something you believe in.

the uncertain promise
of the years to come.

the unhurried pleasure of a long walk
through the streets of new york.

the exquisite disquiet
of the benevolent whisper.

the simple art of living life
on your own terms.

the reverence of that one person
who never let you down,

and the profound privilege of living
in this world with you.

for you

i think about you all the time.

i think about you even when
we're together.

i hear your voice still,
your first words
and your last words,
and your first words again.

i still remember your weight in my arms
on our first night
between wakefulness and dreaming.

and after the lights were unplugged,
and the needles had fallen off the trees,

it was you who made
every table more elegant,
every day more civilized,

and life was filled
with more brilliance
than ever could be imagined.

and this certainty
fills me with my first hope
of remembering you.

possibility

try to live life with an easy rhythm
of spontaneous kindness

and always love
with the heart of youth.

languidly forge deep meanings with
the modest, but not the falsely modest.

and embrace limitless freedom
so that you have nothing to prove
and nothing to regret.

remember there will always be
death and decay,
but there will also
always be
the possibility
for grace and beauty.

centuries

as paris sighs and new york sleeps,
i am reminded that the world
has still not learned to love properly
after all these centuries.

the fragile elements

living as austerely as possible
with unblushing brilliance,
untouched radiance,
unresolved endings,
unfinished stories,
and words left unsaid.

these fragile elements
will still fuel
the flared hope
of romance
and history
and authenticity.

so never stop
striving for serenity
and good manners,
and a humility
that is
beyond contestation.

for alan

alan had down syndrome,
and he was my best friend.

we grew up on the same block,
playing baseball and stickball
in the summer,
football and hockey
in the winter,
but basketball was alan's favorite.

he would come to my house
bouncing his ball, and
we would walk together
to the nearby schoolyard.

the schoolyard separated my neighborhood
from a broken block of housing projects
and occasionally the two would meet.

they would make fun of him
with the usual names,
filled with all the hatred of youth,
and after a few exchanged words,
i would throw the first punch
without thinking twice.

a few cut lips and the occasional black eye,
but i figured the pain in alan's heart
was worse than all the bruises and scratches
my body could withstand.

during many of the fights,
alan would stand to the side,
and i would hear him nervously say:
"oh man...oh man,"

but it was ok.

when it was over,
and the bullies ran away,
which they always did,
alan would look at me
with just a smile
and a hint of victory.

i didn't say anything and neither did he.

we would pick up where we left off,
and the rest of the day was ours.

alan always had a runny nose
and a little saliva dripping
from his lower lip, which he would wipe
with his bare hands all over the basketball.

it was a little annoying at first,
but i got used to it over time.

he would also always greet me
with a near-suffocating hug,
so everything else was easily overlooked.

we would play for hours.

alan had a hard time differentiating
time and memory, so he continued to show up at
my parents' house asking if i was home and if i
could come out and play - long past the time i
left for college, and for many years after.

yet every time i returned home, he would
somehow arrive at just the right moment,

and we would walk off
and play basketball.

when we were young, any time i happened to be in
the local paper after a game, alan would cut out
the article and show it to me.
he always asked me to bring my basketball -
he said it was good luck and a magical ball.

the last time we played together,
i flipped it to him and told him to keep it.

he said,
"i always wanted this,"
and gave me another bear hug.

he got so excited that he ran
down the street with both hands wrapped around
the ball yelling:
"i have to show my mom. i have to show
my mom."

as i watched him run awkwardly down the street,
i knew i wouldn't be able to repeat
the brilliance of that afternoon.

when i think back to the moments of my youth,
it is alan that remains painted on my mind.

and when i think about life,
and who comes in and who goes out
and what they represent,

alan, to me,
was simply the remnant of hope

who emerged
and receded
and resurfaced
at all the right moments.

i haven't seen him now in about five years.
i'm 41 years old,
and his memory alone has sustained me.

i am thankfully unburdened by regrets
and the passage of time.

perhaps the value
of holding on to things isn't so much
about wanting the past to come back,
but more about
wanting to keep remembering it,
fondly and warmly.

thank you alan.

blood and effort

i open my arms
to the evening sky
to grab an instance
of grace,
of tenderness,
of hope.

i whisper to myself:
give me youth.
give me adulthood.
give me old age.

i push past
the proud doors
hiding the secrets of ruins.

i push past
the old neighborhoods giving way,
dissolving before our eyes,
as new buildings,
taller than before,
lift up the sky.

i push past
the local stores opening and closing.

i push past
the new generation of moving boxes
piled high on the street.

and i run straight

the silence between what i think and what i say

to the glorious failures
and splendid imperfections

with the remembrance
that blood and effort will
always defeat
style and talent.

life lived right

fill the spaces
between what you see
and what you know.

become a radiant example
for how to really live.

embrace the fragility
that surrounds you
day in and day out.

and look back
to discover
the immediacy
of that long-forgotten moment.

let the tears rise up in you,
and do everything you can
between today
and the day of your last breath.

the future eloquently
awaits you to live your life.

and if lived right,
it will always demand
a great amount of bravery.

so put all you have into it
and give up on all else

the silence between what i think and what i say

        that doesn't deserve
        your
        tireless
        exquisite
        effort.

let us re-enact
our exhausted love

let us say what was left unsaid.

let us touch what was left untouched.

let us put a little magic
back into this life.

let us fully experience
what is right before our eyes.

and let us have
a few more nights
of peaceful anonymity,

where in the extraordinary way
things happen,

time will pass,

circumstances will change,

and it will all dissolve
into unbreakable intimacy
with simple gestures
of love and devotion.

everything will surrender to time, except...

with luck and a little effort,
i will whisper these words
through sun-filled windows
to privately record
these very particular moments,
scribbling across the arc of a lifetime.

i will expect little or nothing from the public.

i will stay as unpretentious as possible.

and i will ask
for an audience of family and friends
who will find
these words
written below a heart
that only beats for them,
in a home still filled with youth
and endurance

where everything will surrender to time,
except my love for you.

art & love

each word must
be written
with the greatest of truthfulness,

and each love
must be given
with the greatest of tenderness.

floating and treading
in the atlantic

swimming out
past the surfers,
who become silhouettes
against the light

together again,
floating
and
treading
in the atlantic

squinting into the sun

forgetting the weight of burden
and the blood of tragedy

dreaming of
the partnership
we hope
will keep us safe
in an unsafe world.

the answers to the secrets

in the middle of the crowd,
your solitude
will be your sanctuary.

give women what they want:
kindness and equality
and to always feel beautiful.

remaining sincere
will almost seem
like an act of courage.

strive for a general goodness
free of religious persuasion.

keep your sense of fragility
but don't sacrifice your strength.

when they tell you
to settle down and
be responsible,
stay free and
embrace the whirlwinds,
because you actually
don't grow by success;
it's failure where the lessons lie.

engineer your life
so that you don't have to wait
for the weekends,
and live
so that you can spend

the majority of your time
writing a few
undeniable sentences,
capturing that moment
in a photograph,
or surrendering in the arms
of your one true love.

and when you get a little lost
along the way,
which you certainly will,
try to remember the good things
and always believe that
something pure can last.

II.

the soundtrack of the city
becomes a lover's refrain
heard through the centuries . . .

a glimpse of a disappearing way of life

a moment stirred by laughter,
a piece of forgotten music,
a true sensation of kindness,
eyes full of trust,
the slow beat of your heart on top of mine,
words whispered in the dark of night,
the splendid shadow of your spirit,
the unapologetic beauty of your intimacy,
the exquisiteness of your face in the morning
and the quietness after.

i will write these words for you
and keep them pressed
between the pages of my youth
marked by triumph,
inspired by courage.

with this,
i wonder what is the secret
behind the blue light of the night sky.

the riveting light
i kissed you under for the first time.

i look to the face of this same light
when the moon is rising
and the sun is resting.

the light that allows me to capture
a moment of you in a photograph.

the light that wraps around my hands
as my hands wrap around you,

the silence between what i think and what i say

and the light
that provided us with grace
on that first morning
when we surrendered to each other.

my heart beats faster
for the sweetness of this memory,

and i am left
with a howling breathlessness
that rises above the struggle
to reach the victory that is you.

when i die

have something genuine
and simple, if possible.

bring me singing and weeping.

do not sanitize my body.
do not comb my hair.
do not color my face.

look at my dead body,
and when you do,
you will be looking at your own absence.

turn away
and live the way it was intended
through the centuries.

look closely enough,
and you may find some truth.
and you may find that love is all there is.

and when you look at this dead body again,
realize that the heart has stopped
and this is the last
you will ever see of me.

but remember that
my heart stopped
1,000 times before.

now let me rest.

the silence between what i think and what i say

only ever, looking forward

keep the tone peaceful,
the mood happy,
the night good,
the instincts hopeful,
the influence pure,
the gallantry genuine.

keep an educated eye on
authentic intimacy
and the struggle
to remain private.

let your bewilderment
subside into exhausted relief.

keep the spectacular chaos of your days
filled with emotions
and still-formulating ideas,
but be able to suppress the chaos
in favor of any immediate concerns.

become the enviable solution
to the ever-growing demands
of life and work
in middle age,
and search for beauty
that barely uses any words

it will be sacred.
it will be delicate.
it will be silent.

don't you know

don't you know
that what we have
shines
proudly and brilliantly?

don't you know
that we have a chance
to live
like no one's ever lived before?

don't you know
that what i miss most
are your eyes
as you look back at me
on your way to work
with that proud step
i always remember?

don't you know
that you still remain
the constant presence in my life?

and don't you know
that you will forever occupy
that honored place in my memory
like a favorite movie,
an afternoon drive,
a summer song
and a first kiss?

i also believe...

that ambition is ungracious.

success is a substitute for luck.

there is more to life than the weather report.

not every person wants to be a celebrity and
not everyone runs to stand in front of a camera.

relationships fade more often than necessary.

if you feel like saying i love you, then say it.

if you feel like holding hands, then do it.

look past the blur of uniformity
and continue the search for
a retreating beauty amid the world's disruptions,
despite the fact that
america still finds it difficult
to grow old
and is incapable of having an
unapologetic appreciation
for leisure,
sincere desires,
indelible moments of grace,
and belief in the grandeur
of small gestures.

i will continue
to pray to the gods
that i'm quite sure don't exist.

stephan silich

ode to new york

new york is a tiny island,
and perhaps you can't fit
all these dreams
in such a tight space.

but i never came here
for dreams or reinvention.

i was born here, raised here,
lived my whole life here,
and will most likely die here.

and so
this eternal city
trembles with decadence,
constantly moving
and changing
and drifting
and renovating
and restoring
and tearing down
and building up.

everyone seeking
something prettier
and newer
and faker,
as hopes shiver
in the shadow of a desperate cry.

but something happened
along the way.

your closeness
made me see the city
in a different light,
and i have been
squinting into the sun
ever since.

this golden light
will make you forget
the lack of truth and
howls of pain.

instead,
it will bring a few
moments
shimmering across
the ravages of time.

many in this city
have access to privilege;

the key is to not access it,
but to revel
in the sweetness of doing nothing.

look for the
harmonious rows of limestone townhouses
and cast-iron downtown lofts.
look across the green fields of central park,
past the flower markets and cafes,
the tree-lined streets along the hudson,
and the immensity of grand central,
surrounding us with unknowing drama.

i see
stargazers
and thinkers

and dreamers
seeking inspiration
in the steps of cobblestones
and in the glimmer of street lights,
as the soundtrack of the city
becomes a lover's refrain,
patiently surveying
the vastness of the landscape
with a refined eye.

and you'll have to discard
your notes of complaint
and your pages of protest

because
restaurants become photographs,
benches become sculptures,
terraces become songs,
sidewalks become canvases,
rooftops become love letters.

swooning and embracing together
with the muted splendor of discovery
and near perfect fragility
as we fall into states
of lasting euphoria.

friends and lovers,
boyfriends and girlfriends,
husbands and wives,
parents and children,
brothers and sisters,

linger
with an extra cup of coffee

to keep these
rapturously beautiful
moments
just that:

beautiful.

remember,
new york is not really
a beautiful place,
but it's a place
that occasionally has beautiful things in it.

where
bridges become words,
lampposts become embraces,
trains become conversations,
buildings become encounters,
and hotels become magical
in the middle of the night,
making you remember
that there is something peaceful
about knowing the people you love
are sleeping soundly in their beds.

it holds all the strength and romanticism
of the feminine world
with its nurturing purity,
distant gazes,
reticence,
and raptures of tenderness.

the slow spin
of carriage wheels
making their way
past the storefront windows,
the street vendors

the community gardens
and the dog walkers,
as leaves tumble
in a breeze of change.

remember
that the richness
is in the human details,
in lived-in faces,
uneven voices
and slightly crooked smiles.

look
how the buildings
meet the sky,
and you will be given
a suggestion of mortality
and a heart that no longer
strains to be heard.

give me anguish.
give me euphoria.
give me dignity.
give me restraint.
give me comfort.
give me sadness.
give me strength.

give me bravery
through naked declarations.

give me all the
bursts of emotion
and flares of exhaustion.

but also give me
the poetry of stillness,

and let it stretch out across infinity.

for you are the tear in my tear flow,
the heart in my heartache.

it is the ideal backdrop for our love,
and this has been
an exquisite love story
from the start.

a story
about a place that continually draws
the map of my heart,
which still beats
recklessly and loudly,
unquestioned and undimmed,
with every moment,
every perspective,
every impulse,
and every desire,
shared and remembered.

it is about a boy who loved a girl.

a boy who had no ambition in life
other than to cover
every inch of her body
with his lips.

a love never to be abandoned
and never to suffer
the pains of vanished beauty.

remember
that in the course
of history,

there always comes a time
when humanity is given hope.

and i will remember
our kiss
under the slow moon.

i will remember
how your presence
fills me with all i need.

i will remember
the years of tenderness
that will cover the trail
of life's sorrow.

i will remember the gentle lull
of the contented heart,

and i will remember
these sweet words
spoken to you only
as day melts into twilight.

the sweetest thing

the first beautiful thing
is the sweetest thing,
and the sweetest thing
is seeing your face
in the morning light,
which is always a little unsettling
because at some point,
we'll separate for the day.

but i know that time holds no constraint
in the quest to capture memory,
and i remember how your heart felt
beating in my hands,
as each beat brought me closer to you.

i am still bewildered by the recognition that
in this strange and strangely hopeful place,
i found you.

it is not every day that we are needed,
and i mean truly needed.

but today,
at this time,
in this moment,
i need you.

new york 2012

i choose to live here,
even though
i can't see everything i want to see.
but i know the key is to no longer
feel an obligation
and just enjoy whatever small fraction
happens to find you.

so i keep close, but just out of reach,
in these streets that we love and hate,
alongside wide-eyed tourists
and restless locals.

tired of an indifferent place
but still pushing through this veil of time,
allowing the songs of the world
to shout forth through enfolding darkness.

these naked verses of youth,
long sought and hard won,
speak to us of love and hope and romance
because in this city,
every window is a lens
and every street is a photograph.

across time and space

the new york night
was young and beautiful
when we first met.

as i contemplated
the elegance of falling rain,
your calm,
warm laughter
provided me
an authentic expression of decency
and a guide to remain
tenderly empathetic to solitude.

and now,
with these winter nights upon us,
we avoid the cold with each other's arms
and lie on our sides,
my naked back
against your pregnant stomach,
as the muted kicks of our unborn daughter
offer the magical promise of life,
which will be treated with special care
and make up for some
of what we have suffered.

we look
into each other's eyes
as if every breeze in the night air
is a whisper for her alone.

and the beauty of keeping love
across time and space
will be ours.

native son

a hymn to freedom,
a hymn to love,
a hymn to those who wander this city
admiring how the moon
makes her way through
the downtown streets.

searching for my place,
i stopped here for coffee,
i stopped there for wine,
continuing through landscapes
and across destinations unplanned.

your native son
asks for your embrace
amidst the sweet sadness
and tragic nobility
of this lonely place -
this lovely spy of harsh beauty.

but your native son
also asks forgiveness
for cursing you
and wanting to leave you
more than anything in the world

because sincerity
always triumphs over pretension.

because one should never be shocked
by an expression of genuine emotion.

because there is indeed a time for everything.

because the future does rest
on the evocation of the past.

because ambition and impatience
should not be considered virtues,
and because love looks not with the eyes..

so what is the reward for this solitude?

time regained?

an echo of memory?

i'm not sure,
but i do know that
everything that will happen to you
will happen today.

so slow down.

quietly close your eyes to see.

let wisdom in.

let nostalgia rise in its own time.

don't get tired.

she is approaching you,
resplendently,
and you will choose her
over all others.

for emma
(from your mother and father,
written by your father, august 2013)

there are only a few things,
a very few,
on the face of this earth
that render me awestruck.

and one,
without question,
is the face of my
6-month-old daughter.

her simple,
calm,
bouncing smile
contains all of life's definitions:

mercy,
glory,
truth,
tenderness,
redemption,
humility,
integrity,
toughness,
beauty,
strength,
honesty.

emma,
after 43 years,
my lifelong search for meaning
has been realized in you.

please know that you
and your mother
are with me in all my dreams
and in all my waking moments.

we can only hope you are held
the way you want to be held
because you are beautiful at all times.

you were born
from a relationship of love and kindness,
and it is with love and kindness
that you will grow.

we don't know how to measure the distance
between the world we know
and the world we want for you,
but we do know that
because of you
everything is filled with possibility.

and because of you,
we are certain that
the small sum of tender gestures
will bring about the noble
and sincere pursuit
of being your father
and mother
and friend.

and although
you cannot yet speak to us with words,
we speak to you
with the gentlest of whispers,
every night
and every morning,

stephan silich

when we lean close,
kiss your cheek,
and say:

we love you.
we love you.
we love you.

some advice to get you through

whether inhaling
the smells of nearby bread stands
or welcoming
the solitude of late summer,
these are the moments
during the day,
and during the night,
that help navigate
a world of despair mixed with
a world of sudden beauty.

remember the familiar places -
those are the ones
that hold a certain magic,
especially when the memories are shared.

embrace the unassuming and unaffected
way to be feminine:
little makeup,
not much jewelry,
nothing fake.

beauty that stands on its own
and doesn't long to be stared at.

beauty that gently reminds us of truth.

be the kind of man
whose face and actions
warrant a pause, not a faint.

keep your grace
by staying out of the public's attention,

and remain at the edge of all things
surrounded by the barest glow of candlelight.

subtlety
will extend one's appreciation,
and a sensitive restraint
will give you the proper amount of time
to take it all in.

if you go out for dinner,
talk about romantic love
and the nostalgia for lost times.

authentic emotions will endure,
and compassion will bring kindness;
kindness will bring empathy;
empathy will allow you
to communicate with the rest of humanity.

quiet the worry from the pressure
of having to do something
and having to be something.

quell the doubt over the kind of career
you will have or won't have;
it simply doesn't matter,
as long as you have a lived life.

silence the outside voices,
and the integrity of the present
will be right in front of you;

this will be your path ahead.

simplicity always wins over sophistication.

stay radiant
but not untouchable.

civilized
but not boring.

graceful
but not pretentious.

allow yourself
to be overcome by emotion
at the sight of your children sleeping,
and acknowledge the parts of yourself
that you keep hidden.

risk revealing the deepest part
to someone you love;
they will most likely respond with kindness.

sincerity and humility
are the only possibilities,
and the only hope.

there is nothing better
than growing old together.

it's easy to destroy something;
for it only takes ten minutes
to cut down a tree
that took a hundred years to grow.

disregard the inclinations
toward a distant past,
and measure your carefree youth
and delicate fascination with beauty
carefully.

accept aging sweetly,
with smile lines suggesting
a sense of dignity.

stay humbled by nature and broken dreams.

if you haven't tried, then you haven't lived.

the little pleasures worth dying for

with the weight of time,
the truth will always rise to the top.
if you walk down the street
under a declining sun,
and the steps are not easy,
make a promise
for a new life.

because if done right,
it will be
a suggestion,
a question,
a statement,
a judgement,
a provocation,
a notion,
a desire,
a protest,
and above all,
a work of art.

never let go
of the memory
of that perfect moment,
or a feeling sensed through a book
or a movie
or a song
or a painting
or the love of a good woman
a kind woman.

if you follow these words,
which i wish you would,

you will most likely
remain open-hearted
while broken-hearted
which is as it should be,
because that's what counts
in the end.

and the true end is always unexpected,
even when expected.

but there is hope in uncertainty,
so don't be afraid of the solitude.

sometimes tremendous effort
yields modest results,
but it is the devotion
that fulfills the meaning.

feel the rush of love
and the surge of grief,
and be aware, at all times,
of the heart that beats,
for it will soon lie still.

don't be afraid to be forgotten.

what will you be thinking in the final moments?

youthful and charming love

raw and anguished intimacy

urban decay

neglected architecture

refined restorations

the relentlessly restless

the sleepy silence

the history of brushstrokes

the air of impermanence

the suggestion of a life in progress

prayers in a cathedral

easy laughter

brief gestures

or

the romantic search for meaning

across the radiant open space of america

as you run past everyone and everything

straight through to life's last day.

remember

the importance of discretion
and the treasure of being alone.

remember,
only a handful of gestures
will recall a life lived.

remember,
it's best not to follow the crowd
or be a leader of masses.

remember,
be brave
and embrace the lonely quest
for unspeakable beauty.

remember,
the ability to listen is an art,
and so is the ability to have a light touch.

remember,
to admit your delicacy
and honor your kindness;
they are not marks of weakness,
but declarations of gallantry,
and the whisper to the world
that you are tender.

remember,
being careful is civilized,
happiness is an achievement,
hope a reward,
and kindness a victory.

remember,
it is ok
to have a feeling
for something that already existed
and a love for something already felt.

remember,
leave a trace of something:
a photograph, a few words, a drawing,
a garden, a clean desk, a made bed.

remember,
time will pass and leave you behind
as sure as the century jogs past history,

and remember,
you may not get the life you wanted,
but as long as you fail
and fail again and again,
it will be just fine
because you have lived.

i am waiting

i am waiting for inspiration and authenticity.

i am waiting to be a man of elegance and discernment,
to be interested in art
and architecture
and literature
and fashion
and photography
and sculpture
and music.

i am waiting for first impressions
not to harden into lasting judgements.

i am waiting for the feeling of gratitude
not to decline into resentment.

i am waiting for everyone to stop failing to see
the magnificence around us.

i am waiting to embrace the notion of permanence
when change is the human condition.

i am waiting for the nobility of intimacy
and the virtues of loyalty.

i am waiting for the retreat from long hot days.

i am waiting for the tenderness of the original.

i am waiting for warmth that wants nothing in return.

the silence between what i think and what i say

i am waiting for a few moments of contemplation
to punctuate the busy, desperate activity
of living in new york.

i am waiting to wake up early
to watch the city rise over the east river.

i am waiting to look through
this familiar place
with windows gazing back at me,
eyes reflecting hope.

i am waiting to
run along new york harbor
where the river flows into the sea,
past vacant piers,
rotting structures,
crumbling bulwarks,
past taverns and warehouses,
past watchmakers,
and booksellers,
and garment workers,
where block after block opens
like an untold, unscripted story,
recalling the beautiful immigrants that once lived here,
dreaming through snow-swept windows
weeping with condensation.

i am waiting to live life
with a sense of relaxed urgency.

i am waiting for the generous well of history
to rise above me
bringing memories of you

that will remain
in the privacy of my heart.

i am waiting for the joyful urgency
of seeing the world through your eyes
and the deep pleasure of sincerity
in the fading afternoon light.

i am waiting for the arc of your life
to be etched into mine.

i am waiting for the wistful glimmer
of undiminished love
and for you to remember me
simply as a time of day.

i am waiting for the occasionally funny
and devastating
last years of our lives.

i am waiting
for the specific moment,
on this specific day,
when time will stand still,
and we are left
with ageless beauty
and timeless relevance.

III.

the remembrance
of spending time in your company
is reason enough
for all the gratitude in the world . . .

open the window please

my 2-year-old daughter
looks out the car's back window
under a cloudless sky and yells:

"open the window please."

as the sudden breeze hits her face,
she shouts:
"the moon . . . the moon . . . look! look!"

how do you compete with this?
how do you even describe this?

to watch life breathe hope from her eyes,
completely unspoiled by perfection,
lends itself to a moment
that at first appears fleeting
but is actually
filled with an air of immortality
that will remain untouched
by the passing of time.

the little ones

my small,
humble,
little icons of beauty,
pure inspirations
of all that is good in the world.

i can only hope you find new life,
every day,
amid the wonders of new york.

you two
are my songs of unconquerable love
and my poems of unbounded compassion

you both have given
meaning to my life
i had absolutely no right
to ever expect.

and i now have this drenching
and glorious experience
of waking up every morning
and saying:

i want nothing more than this day in front of me.

testament

sitting in the midday sun
where light filters through
and reminds one to dream.

these kind of days
have a way of sliding by
less noticed,

so i sit here and write these words,
and you still show up on every page.

i'm trying to compose some kind of testament
to what i remember and what i can no longer recall
or maybe just some sort of elegy
for what i have found and what i have lost.

but i see your face in every memory:
in the blue of sea,
in the green of olive,
in the grey of stone,
in the black of the night sky behind us,
and in the distance ahead of us.

i'm thinking about the losses dealt out by time,
and it reminds me of the nobility of aging monuments,
and it reminds me that privacy is not expected,
but it is certainly appreciated.

and it reminds me that each word and each photograph
will always be different from the next,

the silence between what i think and what i say

because they are imperfectly,
yet lovingly made,
and made just for you.

and this now reminds me
that just enduring this life
is enough of a victory.

begin

there is always a moment,
there is always a little space,
just before the sense of isolation sets in,
and just before the daunting task
of the day begins.

as i start the middle
of the second act
of this mortal play,
i no longer know how
to proceed,
and it haunts my every step.

the elusiveness of time
and the chronological sequence of my heart
no longer form a straight line.

but with the right words,
and the right glance,
and even the right touch,
this life will be
endlessly resistant
to cynicism and clichés.

the invocation
of childhood memories
and the remembrance
of the supreme brilliance
of my parents' love
are all that is needed to get me through.

even now, in my mid-40s,
a simple message
from my mother saying:

"good morning, stephan,
i am always thinking about you
and hope you are enjoying your life.
we love you and want the best for you"

can render me speechless.

the evocative display of beauty
will make you trust your aloneness
so it can no longer defeat you.

and remember what i have said many times before:
you can destroy a man,
but it doesn't mean he is defeated.

so ask yourself,
what is your state of being?
what is the ache at the center of your existence?

find it

and begin.

the art of dying

slightly tired
from a day of walking
through neighborhoods and ancient squares,

i sit and think about
this life,
and this city,
and the noble spirit of the elderly
among timeworn gravestones,
cracked and discolored in places,
imperceptibly whispering wisdom to whomever will listen.

others preceded me here,
that i can tell from the dried lilies left behind.

a few fine oak trees stand nearby,
just beyond
fields and flower gardens,
courtyards and cobblestones,
and playgrounds
where children laugh and chase each other.

our final act
should be our own composition,
but i still want you to give me
a conscious farewell:

leave me a good-bye note.
leave me a final photo.
leave me a parting sign.

leave me heartbreak without reservation.

i've been waiting a lifetime for this.

remember,
you are my day leading into night,

and contained in everything i do
is you,

so all i can offer is a small apology
for life's briefness.

and as the late afternoon sun
wraps these city streets,
the memory
of spending time in your company
is reason enough
for all the gratitude this life can hold.

for mia
(the age of 1)

the unabashed and unapologetic
immoderation of love
i have for my daughters
is enough
and will be all i leave behind.

as i soulfully examine
the meaning of all this:

the success and the failure,
the weeping and trembling
through life,
through work,
through marriage,
through fatherhood.

i recall an article
i recently read
that said the age of 1 is
"the final moment of expressive innocence"
for a child.

and so as my youngest,
mia,
approaches this next month,
all i can do
is watch closely
as she expresses
what she doesn't yet
have words for:

the silence between what i think and what i say

surprise,
worry,
humor,
serenity,
thoughtfulness,
dismay,
anxiety,
confusion,
need,
hope.

at these moments,
i am focusing on
this staggeringly beautiful concept
that i cannot yet
wrap my arms around.

and, at other moments,
i feel an unbearable presence
in myself of something
i cannot yet explain.

i ask,
of no one in particular,
to remain gentle and tender and unafraid.

and
i ask,
again,
of no one in particular,
to give me this privileged intimacy
so i can feel personally heroic.

as they sleep,
i put my hand
to the simple sheets

under which they lie
and close my eyes to the night.

i silently wonder,
what constitutes a good life?

reread the above
and let me engage
in the unrelenting,
essential
pursuit
that defines
and outlines
my life:

a father's love for his daughters.

the arrival

look at my face closely.
you will see
some pain and some sadness
left over from a life lived
not being in much of a hurry.

but, peacefully now,
i'm on the other side
and moving across
the immensity of time
before you and after me.

the weight
of remaining
consistently concerned
about the feelings of others,
staying dedicated to kindness,
pure kindness,
not for rewards or perceptions,
but effortless kindness,
deep-rooted,
unteachable,
where by force of character alone
one can achieve goodness for its own sake.

hope for the fortune
of luck and circumstance,
and it will ease the gradual persistence
and return of
tenderness,
sincerity

and even
loyalty.

continue perfecting the art of being uncalculating
by surrendering to find your place in the world.

go with the small, happy life
filled with human dignity,
awe and inspiration.

rely on the wisdom of ancient ruins
and the seduction of restraint
from the indelible portrait of goodness.

bring back the notion of time and place,
bring back a sense of decorum,
where men and women alike
know exactly what should and shouldn't be said.

give me ashes and bones,
sounds and echoes,
and watch the arrival of intimate possibility
and a little majestic brilliance.

through it all
i've tried to be a good man,
i've tried more than you know,
and i did the best i could with the life i had.

what i leave behind i hope is of some value.

i know these hands
will never hold another,
and they will remain a symbol
of the remarkable alliance
between triumph and tragedy.

life

the life we dream may
sometimes amount to little,
but the life we lead
is everything
because it continues through our existence.

all the promises we failed to keep,
all the plans that went awry,
will be remembered
and forgotten
and remembered again.

and the staggering swiftness
of our hearts
skips a few beats but beats on.

remembering the places we've been
and the things we've found.

remembering the large decisions
and the small details.

remembering the moments
that marked celebrations
and made the map of our life
unfold across these cities
and towns and beaches.

i'll send invitations to the world,
so they can see it all discreetly come together
and gracefully fall apart.

i'll collect my thoughts,
write them down,
read them now,

read them every day,
and ask:

will i attain the measure of my worth?

will i live a life that matters?

will i never count on another day?

will i get caught saying: if only i had known?

will i embrace the moment

whether it's two minutes from now

two days

two weeks

two years

two decades

or will it always be too soon?

school
(september, 2016)

walking my little one to school
as shadows lengthen
across the stone walls
of park avenue,
that tiny hand placed in mine
fills me with the strength needed
to make it through the day.

we make our way 8 blocks north,
as fragments of conversation
trickle through the doorways.

we pass
men cleaning sidewalks
and women ready for work
and dog walkers navigating
and taxis searching
and buses slowing
and construction workers sitting against buildings
having coffee,
buildings like small monuments
breathing life into the city.

i am aware of the imprint of our upbringing,
so i let her walk at her own pace
and allow time to enfold
as she points out new flowers
making their way in prearranged tree boxes.

i watch in amazement
as she catches a glimpse

of the half-moon's reflection
still hanging in the morning sky,
and she yells:
"hello moon, hello moon."

with a kiss and a hug,
i let her go,
always earlier than i expected.

as i walk home,
i ask for a little of that
noble silence the buddhists talk about.

no phone,
no conversation,
just humble,
subtle,
unflinching contemplation
of the passage of time
and the few charming things of life:

the real-time remembrance
of my beautiful little girl
with scraped knees
and blue sneakers
and a pink dress
bouncing down the street,
with a heart of pure gold,
and a soul full of reckless mischief.

easter with emma
(april 15, 2017)

easter sunday morning,
palm beach gardens, florida:

4-year-old emma sleeping in bed.

i am awake beside her in a rocking chair,
not rocking, but feet up on the end of the bed
reading the introduction to rainer marie rilke's
letters to a young poet
6:05 a.m. on the clock.

i think of an article i read recently that said
'90 percent of all the time you will spend with your children
comes before the age of 12'.

this is it then.

a few birds outside,
a low hum from the air conditioner,
and the simple breathing of my little girl.

i put the book down and listened;

43 minutes went by,
the most peaceful of my 47 years.

the art of unsung work

will someone escort me out of this life
when the stunningly intimate time comes?

will my soul be reflected
in the shadows?
in the streets?
in the oceans?

i am aware of the
inescapable impermanence
and solemnity of the occasion,
which will not be lost
on the historical memory
bearing witness to this life,
expressing it
and discussing it
and honoring it all at once.

what matters most
is the art of unsung work,
the serenity left in children,
the private suffering
of graceful human beings
who pass through our midst
and leave us much too soon,
the unendingly moving
and inspiring courage
it takes to get through daily life
without destroying hope
amidst the immutable laws of mortality.

so try loving something
that transcends a lifetime,

some ideal filled
with
honor
and
glory
and
humility.

and remember,
with sweeping gestures unseen,
i will always be with you,
in small rooms mostly,
taking up no space at all.

look past them

when you wake up in the morning,
remind yourself that some of the people
you will work with today will be
dishonest
and
arrogant
and
unhappy.

but remember
they are like this
because
they do not know
the value of kindness,
the wisdom of humility,
the beauty of integrity,
and the worth of dignity.

all very difficult to regain when lost
in the blur of life's everyday demands.

so look past them,
as you will invariably
come across at least one or two people
who are filled
with a nobility
that is honorable
and sincere
and has a certain elegance
that you can't quite explain:

the silence between what i think and what i say

a slight tilt of their head,
the way they hold a coffee cup,
the way they place their hand under their chin,

and most importantly,
the way their eyes catch yours
through the shadows of time and distance.

kindness

here he comes
with gentle wisdom
and disarming warmth,

and i am left with
an expansive awareness
as we share
sacred exchanges
across moments of time:
over breakfast,
over dinner,
over a few drinks.

i am reminded that presence
is infinitely more meaningful
than productivity,
and this languid time,
this inextinguishable luminosity,
will spread
across a lifetime
as our ancestors
sing in our blood,
and their spirit carries us through the ages.

tell me again about your childhood.
tell me again about your parents.

show me your unquestionable strength again,
your monogram of fortitude
without limits.

thank you.

give me a three word description:
venerable
austere
elegant.

give me reflections of timelessness.

give me the weight of expectation.

give me indiscernible resignation and recompense.

let me know if mankind
can start anew
because i am sure
we will be granted
one last gasp of beauty before death.

glimpsing now
what no mirror can reflect,
my soul shoots out
across the night sky
because of your delicate
and deliberate
acts of kindness.

thank you again.

for pop

stage four.
there is no stage five.
a breath away.
everyone has to do this at one point or another.

out of reach and
within reach
at the same time.

the terrible exhaustion
has arrived for you,
so i pray for serenity and temperance.

the unaccustomed stillness
in your aging body
brings forth
the realization of the
appurtenances of illness
that are all around you:

the large pill box,
the medication logs,
the lotions,
socks,
sweatshirts,
hairbrush,
tissues,
moisturizers,
lip balm,
heating blanket.

and i see all the
appurtenances of youth:
little emma and mia - right across from you -
surrounded by
their dolls,
toy horses,
unicorns,
pink dresses,
plastic keys,
bows for their hair.

the two mix well.

so well,
that all of life
is right here in front of us
in this moment,
in this house,
at this table.

our 76-year-old
father and grandfather,
working on a puzzle of animals
with our little girls.

watching as they
learn to be patient,
exploring what may work,
and figuring out what doesn't
and searching for what may fit
and struggling for what may not.

they achieve,
they fail,
and like all of us,
they learn the only way out
is straight through.

the drama of their youth begins.
the drama of your life begins.

and word after word
and line after line
and page after page
and chapter after chapter
and book after book,
time passes
and yet stays still.

preparations are made
for dying and living.

the belief of what a family should be
was learned from you
and will never diminish.

we are your sons,
and we send a warm salute
with a wave of gratitude to
the woman
who gave birth to us.

take a bow dad.
take a much-deserved bow.
your sons are grateful for you.

your sons love you.

you are the measure of all things.

the vividness and the memorableness
that is you is here.
it is here now.
it will not dim.

we will relive the grandeur that was you.

and i assure you,
that you may only be reading the voice of one
crying through these words,
but i am the voice of many.

get some rest pop.

get some rest.

we will see you tomorrow.

IV.

the bomb waits in the warehouse
and the razor reveals the face's truth . . .

the smile

i was headed home
from work
and waiting at a red light
when i looked up and
saw my mother's car
making a right turn
on the other side of the street.

our eyes met,
and she gave me
the warmest smile
i had ever seen,
and a little wave of her hand,
as we both
continued on
our separate ways.

it was undeniably magical.

celebrate

most of our lives are not
what we want them to be,
and it reminds
me of what an
old college professor
once told me:

"even the best
possible effort
may not meet with
the success it deserves."

it's why
we read these books,
listen to this music,
stare at these paintings,
touch these sculptures,
develop these photographs,
and search for the one we never find.

it is why
i write these words
on these pieces of paper
and celebrate
these small victories,
like a celebration
of your first love
and how that haunts
you forever.

the blind side of your soul

someone somewhere is writing words with a pencil
along the edges of old napkins,

someone somewhere is sitting on a terrace
sculpting marble until his fingers bleed,

and someone somewhere is dripping a little life
onto an empty canvas with broken paint brushes.

if you get this,
then i can assure you that
the drudgery
and the dullness
and the difficulty of life
will escape right through
the blind side
of your soul.

out the front door

i'm not rich and i'm not famous.

i'm happy.

i'm just trying
to get some of these words
down on paper
while remaining
faithful and patient,
humble and pure.

if you listen
carefully,
you can hear
the lamentations
from the abandoned piers
across the city's edge,
where love
once rested.

and you will realize
the noble gesture in living.

and when you
walk out the front door
in the morning,
you should be able
to smile at all you see.

no heat

no heat
in the apartment
tonight,
and the
super
just told me
it's going
to be like this
for a few more days.

with my right hand
i write these words,
as my left hand
rests on top of the desk light,
its radiant heat
warming my entire body.

there is a certain brilliance
to nights like this,
and there's a certain brilliance
in bursting into tears
at unexpected moments.

i wouldn't trade this
for anything in the world.

the silence between what i think and what i say

the wordless portrait

when i was in college,
i took a course called
"artists' lives on film."

there were about 15 of us
in the class,
and it basically consisted
of sitting around a tv
watching documentaries
and short films
on some of the greatest artists
of our time.

i was introduced to:

rembrandt and goya
van gogh and gauguin
picasso and matisse
pollack and basquiat.

but the main attraction
was my teacher.

she was in her late 50s,
and she would wear
these big round glasses
that partially shaded her eyes,
and she wore long brown skirts
that hung tight
around her full hips.

i would catch her
daydreaming
in the tv light
as the words and images
seemed to magically appear
on the screen.

when the lights came on,
she would stand
in front of her desk
and describe the films
and the artists
and their artwork
and life in general
with statements like:

"his life was a collision of a wish
and an unyielding reality."

"it is by finding out what something
is not that one comes closest to
understanding it."

"we are injured most by what we do
not expect."

"external circumstances do not reflect
internal qualities."

"you can see the troubled emotions
encased with ambitious ideas."

"the destinies of men
are controlled by the gods."

"what makes us angry
is our dangerously optimistic notions
about people and the world."

"the spectacular chaos of our days
will be importantly present in the
middle of our lives."

i used to write down these words
on the edges of my notebook.
and think of her often.

on the last day of class,
our eyes met
and she must have
known my thoughts
because
i could see her
trying to hold back
a smile.

and just before
class was over
she said

"remember one of the most
beautiful things in the world
is the gaze of the viewer
from one detail to another."

and as our eyes met again,
she said thank you.

i responded the same
and headed out the door.

you will find it right there

go on
too long
and
death
will
seem
the
kindest
thing.

so
run past
the fishermen
pulling
in their
nets
as
earth
slips away
from the
sun

and watch
as their backs
bruise
again
and
again.

run past
the revolutions
and
the wars

the factories
and
the coal mines.

run past
the fear
that
has
languished
in your soul
for
eternity.

run past
the exhausting perfection.

run past
the relentless
pursuit
of
beauty

and you
will
find
it
right there
in the soft
features
of her
face

and
it will
remain there
in

those unknown
lives
around
you

and
she will
stay
with
you

under
the lonely sky

inside
plaster-filled walls

across
sleeping villages

above
buried workers
from fallen cathedrals
and
directly
into
the
afternoon
sun.

the silence between what i think and what i say

as i write from bed on a monday night

the bluebird sits on the windowsill.

the lion licks his paw.

the doctor goes on vacation.

the lover buys new underwear.

the madman checks himself out.

the landlord collects the rent.

the hunter reloads.

the maid opens the curtains.

the tv falls off the shelf.

the bomb waits in the warehouse

and the razor reveals the face's truth.

today

will this be the day you put your shoes on for the last time?

will this be the day you walk straight into her arms?

will this be the day you smell the tragedy of the factories?

will this be the day you become an honest witness?

will this be the day you lift the shades on all the windows?

will this be the day when there will be simply nothing left?

will this be the day, however brief, that stays with you

through the first draft of your obituary?

i don't know.

but i do know

that whatever you do,

just do it with a bravery

that will move them to tears.

the silence between what i think and what i say

through my soul

walk with me
through the downtown streets
and past
the small stores
that keep us together.

the open windows
that let us spy on our neighbors.

the desperate fire escapes
holding on for dear life.

the comfortable sidewalks
at the beginning of day.

the brave stones
of our bridges and museums.

the concrete
on the shoulders of men
who thrust this city upward.

and those buildings
outside our window
that surround time
and history
and memory,
will continue to fill everything
with a fullness that

burns through our existence,
almost the same way
you burn straight through my soul.

the silence between what i think and what i say

keep going

at this very moment
i was thinking to myself
how beauty so often
has to fight
for its existence,
and then you arrived,
and you suddenly
became my
gentle disturbance
on an early friday afternoon.

in our sleep,
i inch my way closer and closer
so that my back touches yours
as we drowsily enter our dreams,
incessantly trying
not to fall in love
while knowing full well
the history of mankind.

i lie here
in this room
with one bed and one bath,
where i write these words,
and where i think of you
and how we first kissed
on that early morning
next to the sluggish ocean.

and because of you,
i will wake tomorrow
with the courage to keep going.

my lost summer

this is my lost summer
when i studied alone,
ate alone,
slept alone,
and sat at my desk alone,
though i was surrounded
by bookshelves upon bookshelves.

all my favorites were there,
the great ones
the heavyweights
from
hemingway to miller
kerouac to bukowski
whitman to steinbeck
faulkner to fante
melville to fitzgerald.

all of them,
by the way,
have been spared this
american tragedy
that i now find myself
trapped in,
with no apparent
mode of escape
at the present time.

but they got me through.
just seeing their names
in the leather bindings

and glancing at the titles
of their blood work:

the sun also rises,
stand still like the hummingbird,
the desolation angel,
betting on the muse,
leaves of grass,
the winter of our discontent,
as i lay dying,
the wine of youth,
tender is the night,
enchanted isles.

just the titles alone
are enough
to make a man weep.

and it got me through.

those and the boy
across the street
with the bouncing ball.

every day
at the same time,
i would hear a ball bouncing
outside my window.

at first,
it was terribly distracting,
but as i looked out
through the wooden blinds,
i saw him.

he was about 7 or 8 years old,
and he bounced a blue ball
against his garage door nonstop.

he appeared happy
and seemingly content,
but he was alone -
not in the companion sense of being alone,
but in the spiritual sense.

he would bounce the ball
off the garage door
and try to have it bounce back
within the square cement blocks
in front of him,
and he would keep at it
until it hit his imaginary box every time.

there was something
about this little guy
that made me tough it out.

perhaps it was his perseverance
or perhaps it was the fact
that he had on two different shoes:
one black,
one brown.

whatever it was,
i thank them:
the little one outside
and the great ones inside.

and regardless of the outcome,
i want to thank them all
for the time we spent together
that summer.

the silence between what i think and what i say

a note from my mom

i woke up this warm july morning
to find a note from mom on the kitchen table.

it simply read:

"good luck. no matter what, you will always be loved, and
you must remember that you are one of a kind. i admire
you and all that you stand for. i am very proud to be
your mom, and i know that sounds corny and i am biased,
but believe me, you are truly special, and you are here
on this earth for a special reason. i love you.
you make me happy to be your mom."

i am rendered silent.

how do you even respond to this?

i'll start with a thank you.

thank you mom, the greatest poet of all time.

all that is good in the world is reflected in your eyes.

and as my soul continues
to search for something i cannot name,
these words will be all i need.

my victory

my victory
will be
surviving
these winter nights
without you.

i live with
a museum of memories
of what could have been,
and sometimes
memory lasts longer
than anything else.

for you were the one
who gave me that night -
that one night,

and i've written about that night before
and how we were alone in that restaurant
and how you sat across from me
in front of the fireplace
during those
waning days of december.

i remember the
tan blouse you wore
and how it opened
from your shoulder
to the corner of your elbow,
and the dream of your skin

began and ended in that small space
which became my dream of you.

it's the only thing
calling for me,
and i'm afraid it will
continue
until you return to me
until
and
until
and
until again.

window seat 15a

july 10th
2004
8:28 p.m.
on a plane above the atlantic,
watching the sun descend behind
clouds 39,000 feet in the sky,
traveling 500 miles per hour.

i continued to dream out the window
as lightning flashed beneath us.

and to think, minutes earlier,
i was in an airport terminal,
where people from all over the world
are brought together
in steel and metal spaces -
not really communicating,
but sharing an experience
of commerce and entertainment,
romance and longing,
fear and anxiety,
while greeting past lovers,
welcoming back sons from war,
connecting flights to honeymoons,
gathering for funerals,
returning from vacations,
leaving home and going home -

all within this
american afternoon.

it is the sum of all possibilities
and the source of all value.

the glamorous outlaw

i am haunted
by the
aching
awareness
of our time
on earth.

i yearn for
the poet wanderer
and the glamorous outlaw
and the beautiful daydreamer
who have left
the accepted notions
of home and safety

heading instead
to the open road,
the city rooftops,
the outdoor courtyards
and the public libraries

gathering life
from every direction
along the underside
of desperation
and euphoria.

scribbling words
into notebooks,

words whose
meaning

cannot be found
but remain essential
to your spirit
when those dreams decay
on cold winter nights

and before
you lie beside me
for one last night of closeness
on one last condensed day of love.

in the midst of life

do you know
that when i leave you and return home,
what i am most aware of
is the silence left behind by your absence?

do you know
that i choose to be alone,
completely alone,
so that you will possibly come back to me?

do you know
that the difficulty of my days
are manageable because of you?

do you know
that i want my hours to be filled
with the sound of your voice?

do you know
that what we have
has absolutely no distance?

and do you know
that right now,
in the midst of this life,
there is only you.

an old man's life

i waited for answers
in those rooms,
those overpriced,
undersized
new york rooms
where i spent so many nights
counting the holes in the
plaster-filled walls from the
now-removed picture hooks.

i thought of the first photograph
i hung there,
in between the peeling paint,
and how it always
kept me company.

most of us know how to be young
but never quite figure out
how to grow old,
especially with solitude
being so much a part
of an old man's life.

but when i reach that point
and become burdened with
a loss for words,
i will
think of you
and how that one night
i watched
as cigarette smoke

the silence between what i think and what i say

curled through the soft light
above your face,

and everything
you were to me
was realized.

V.

i am still looking for
that small window of time
when night becomes day . . .

the secret

search for kindness.

search for the one
who is more than your equal,
and something infinitely sacred
may just be attained,
some small degree of perfection
may actually be possible.

and in this place,
you will find that the fullness of time
is incomparable in its reach.

it's been my thought
that at the end of human life
you reach something essential,
perhaps a kind of simplicity
that is brought about
by old age
or the significance
of a final message.

however, it is possible,
and more importantly,
preferable,
to reach this place earlier rather than later,
but it will involve nothing less than

earnest emotion, serious thought,
and some ethical commitment.

this way,
the message will be properly absorbed,
the invisible deciphered,
the unattainable foreshadowed,
and the inexhaustible unadorned.

it will also require you
to reject
life's frenetic spinning wheel.

and with that comes
the possibility of conquering
the coming day with
effortlessly compassionate eyes.

without exaggeration,
without agenda,

i am now drifting
through time and space
in an unhurried search
just for this

and just for you.

i am still

i am still dealing
with words that once said love
but never meant love.

i am still counting
the times when something comes up
during the day
that i want to share with you.

i am still learning
that you are important enough
for me to worry again.

i am still looking
for that small window of time
when night replaces day.

i am still breathing
a more exalted air
because of you.

and i am still hoping
to conquer the coming day
with the courage you gave me
in the middle of each night
we spent together.

the silence between what i think and what i say

no one will know

the last flower

the last river

the last breath

the last blink of time

and the luminous eloquence

that awaits us all

will wait for me

and i will not fight one minute of it

because no one will ever know

the immeasurable beauty

i have already seen.

all i remember

you made the painful nights less painful,
and just looking at you made me feel better.

so when you ask me not to forget you,

i can only respond:

"you're all i remember."

a life without vulgarity

the attempt to live a life without vulgarity
pushes forth with burning patience
as i drown in sadness knowing someone else's
child grows in the warmth of your belly.

enough sadness to create unbearable silence.

this deception reminds me
that we must choose our first lover carefully,
or the opposite will arrive
urgently, uninvited and visible.

in time,
we will anonymously
be absorbed into earth,
leaving behind truth
but also
a brief instant of purity
in a world of indifference.

with bruised hopes and shades of exhaustion,
the quest continues because life continues.

i'll open my arms to the world now,
an hour at a time,
with palms turned upward,
and remain committed to
this pain
this paper
this pen
this life.

under the low winter sun

the violent promise of time
remains as i search for my place
under the low winter sun.

my soul blinks,
languishing
just before i retire
to my small room
in the city of new york

where i rejoice in
childhood and fearlessness,
strength and decency,
poetry and truth,
and your smile
that still remains
like 1,000 candles
crushing darkness
and making life
decently bearable.

one-room apartment

it's nice to live
in a one-room apartment,
stretched out on the bed
in the dark,
working on a bottle of wine,
with low radio music
in the background.

paper.
pens.
pencils.
notes.
finished poems.
unfinished poems.

burned-out light bulbs.
clean t-shirts.
clean sheets.
backed-up sink.
small photograph of my parents.

light from the alley
breathing through the window.

horns blowing.
men yelling.

typewriter broken.
computer frozen.

2:17 a.m.

i reach
for my last sip,

see your number
scribbled on a piece of paper
waiting by the phone,

and i know
i'll be human again.

for my brother

your existence thunders
through the streets,

and you are at once
the warmth of the kitchen,
the unadorned truth,
the statue's marble,
the appraising eye,
the sheet of music,
the glorious shadow,
the painted canvas.

your existence thunders
through the streets,

and even the end of your cigarette
is more beautiful
than the day's sunset.

outside the morgan library
on 36th and madison

i find myself glancing
at your ten painted toes
as solitude fades
into evening's darkness
on what once was
a struggling night.

a smile,
a few words,
introductions,
and a promise to call.

i walk home
past the drowsy doorsteps
of these new york apartments,
where life lingers
on uninterrupted hours.

i stare at the clouds
unbuttoned in the sky
and see a section of you.

perhaps
you are the lull between the stars.

and perhaps someday
if the gods are good to us,
we will fade

the silence between what i think and what i say

       into that garden
       at the foot of
       the smiling mountain.

lying on a tar roof above the city

lying on a tar roof above the city,
i dream of drenched pianos
filling harlem's river with tears.

i dream of men sleeping soundly
on the night before they're
sentenced to death.

i dream of women and the long silence
underneath their shivering dresses.

i dream of the dog's paw
being more beautiful than
a lifetime of weeping.

i dream of going unrecognized by
heaven as love drips like rosaries
traced on my eyelids.

lying on a tar roof above the city,
i dream . . .

anonymous

to the anonymous women of the world

the ones who are not models and actresses

the ones who are not newscasters and spokespersons

the ones we glimpse in the back of taxis

the ones we pass breathlessly on the street

the ones we smile at in downtown boutiques as we walk by

the ones we share washing machines with

the ones we see reading on park benches

the ones we stand on movie lines with

the ones we watch drinking wine in outdoor cafes

the ones we sit next to on the blue seats of city buses

the ones who tuck their hair gently behind their ears

the ones who keep men off the cliff's edge -

you are the ones who make heaven stop with half a smile

and you are the silent armies

pushing us through history

with the strength and beauty of ancient rome.

for the girl
with the brown hair, brown eyes,
brown sweater, and brown hat

reading
stories and essays
by henry miller
on a
tuesday morning
until
i see you.

your hand is
placed gently
on your cheek,
strands of
brown hair
cross
your face
and brown eyes,
more beautiful
than
bluebirds
flying at dawn.

how the
scattering
perfume
brings me
faith
as you pass by.

grief's drowsiness
still lasts, but
the aching tenderness

the silence between what i think and what i say

       in the hint of your smile
       carries me through
       the day,
       preventing
       my sorrow
       from folding her wings
       across the sadness of night.

good neighbors

karl was his name,
and he lived next door to
me in connecticut for two
years during my junior and
senior years of college.

it was a
house divided
into four apartments,
and we had adjoining rooms
on the ground level.

he was 88 years old,
had a full head
of crazy white hair
and a face that looked like it
had been through
three world wars.

he always wore
the same khaki pants
and white t-shirt with
a hole in the left shoulder.

he smoked cigarettes
until they
burned down
to his fingers,
which were

the silence between what i think and what i say

stained yellow
and sometimes
scarred red
since he would often fall
asleep with one in his hand.

he slept all day
and drank all night.

some days
a taxi would drop him home
from the
grocery store,
and i would
help him with his bags,
which were always
filled with
clanging bottles,
as we walked
to the door.

sitting
in my apartment,
i would hear
his tv across the hall.

he always
left his door open,
and i would go in
after he fell asleep
and turn off the lights and
the tv
and throw
a blanket over him.

sometimes he would
wake up and say:
"my son,
i'm so glad you
came back to me,"

and then
fall back to sleep.

every so often,
i bought new sheets
for his bed,
extra towels
for his bathroom,
soap,
shampoo,
orange juice,
and some milk
for his stomach.

the last time
i saw him,
i went into his apartment
with a bottle of red wine,
and we drank
and watched
johnny carson together.

i enjoyed how much karl
liked it and how he
smiled so wildly
at the screen.

after the show,

and without warning,
he cleared off his piano,
played
"i left my heart in
san francisco,"
and then
walked to his bed,
plopped down, face up,
and began snoring
louder than both
the piano and the tv.

i turned off his light
and shut the door.

the next day
was graduation,
and i never saw him again.

i think back
to my days
in college,
and karl is what remains.

not the girls,
not the friends,
not the nights out,
not the clubs,
not the bars,
not the beach,
not the dances,
not the sunday brunches,
and not even the literature classes.

just him,

an 88-year-old drunk
who loved
johnny carson,
the piano,
a good smoke,
a good drink,
and a good night's sleep.

i guess
in his own way,
he was
screaming at life,
and i just watched
and took note.

so
this is
for you,
karl,
and
wherever
your tired body
now rests,
know that
i miss you,
old man
and think of you often.

endurance

it is the victory of endurance:
the grocery line,
the next bus,
the job interview,
the sunday paper,
the phone call,
the streets,
the laundry,
the garbage trucks,
the cursing youth,
the shrieks of the subway,
and the unread books.

perhaps
my brown eyes
have faded a bit,
but everything
will be ok
because
among earth's
straining humanity,

i've almost
mastered the tears.

warmed by wine

we make our way
through the streets
to find the morning sun.

reckless
and beautiful
and defiantly poor.

we crush our desire to cry
with the same human words
we have always used.

our celebration of life continues
with no possessions to impress,
no influential friends,
no wealthy patrons.

it's our time
to lie in the sand
and swoon
with a hundred hopes,
putting the trembling kiss
at ease

and doing our best
to spend our nights well,
as the hours pass,

always burning
boundless love.

the beautiful ones

the beautiful ones to everyone else
are usually just that - simply beautiful.

but most of the time,
they're unoriginal beauties,
riding through life
on their perfect nostrils and porcelain teeth.

the beautiful ones to me
are the ones with fire for spirit.

they're the ones who put flowers in
their hair while sitting on park benches.

they're the ones who remain
the world's greatest works of art.

they're the ones who
fill the spaces
between life,
and it's the spaces
between life
that are most important.

miracles

almost every sunday
i walk 171 steps to the roof
of my building
where i sit quietly
looking out onto the city.

i scribble words into this
marble notebook with this pen
and listen to the faint sounds
of the buses below and
the water towers above
while thinking of the memories
behind the peeling paint
of these apartment walls.

it is
in this
heaven
that the miracles are still coming,

and these are the things
one must live
with silently.

and so i choose now
to be silent.

fight

you can give this life
a good run just by fighting it.

and if done right,
it will guide you into your own world
where the writers and painters,
if any good,
will find themselves alone.

reread the history of our civilization
and the biographies of the great ones,
and you will see it this way.

they will work out of cheap hotels
and halfway houses
and asylums
and hospitals
and jail cells
and broken-down apartments.

they continue
unrecognized
unread
and
unheard.

perhaps the simple penalty
of finding immense beauty
in a world where they remain
loners who like company,
rebels who seek to fit in,
and isolated poets looking for an audience.

they,
like death, are
desperate,
but at the same time
full of life
and fighting
to the very end.

the silence between what i think and what i say

brief self-interview

most memorable sound: my mother's slippers across the kitchen floor

most memorable smell: my father's shirts

most memorable sight: my brother sculpting marble on his manhattan terrace

most prized possession: my childhood

scariest moment: girlfriend whispering into my ear "don't break my heart"

bravest moment: having children

most embarrassing moment: don't know yet

most beautiful moment: looking into each other's eyes and both of us knowing

in these hours

the world
is a
better place
after
midnight,
especially
when
it's the beginning
of the last day of
your life.

it is
in
these hours,
when
i have
the chance
to thank you
for the time
you've given me.

it is
in
these hours,
when
i realize
how much
we
have to
endure
just to get through
this life,

the silence between what i think and what i say

                    and
                    it is
                    in
                    these hours
                    when i
                    drink this wine,
                    burn this candle,
                    take this picture,
                    open this book
                    and finish this poem.

for emma & mia

as the year comes to a close,
i lie in bed next to you both,
our little girls,
sleeping sweetly
in this inexhaustible magic.

there is something
about the last days of the year
that feels like
the last hours of night:

delicately subtle,
exquisitely languid.

before the gracefulness of sleep arrives,
full of breathing and dreaming,
i give you the gift
of my tender heart,
with all its humanity,
and this alone
provides us
with glory and dignity,
and the notion that
this pure evening calm
will defeat
sunset's reflection
of time's answer.

the silence between what i think and what i say

are you prepared
for the privilege of living?

are you able to embrace
the fleetingness of humanity?

are you able to see
the flashes of wonder and hope
and the glimpses of
redemption
amid bewilderment
and despair?

are you able to remember that your losses,
your rerouted dreams,
your discarded plans,
your unrepeatable moments,
your gentle invitations,
and your bittersweet goodbyes
are nothing short of
unfolding odes
to mankind
that remain with you
as an intimate archive,
giving you direction
and reminding you,
over and over again:

to pay attention to this moment

to live the questions

to seek silence and stillness

to keep reaching

reaching
always reaching
for mercy and fidelity
while remaining charitable and noble.

i, myself, may be failing,
so i offer these
small creations
to fight immortality
and to try to be
remembered in the best possible way.

i remain haunted
by the disquieting,
unrealized life
of a good person,
and so i dedicate this
to those who
dreamed and never saw their dream realized.
to those who loved and were never fully loved in return.
to those who really took a chance and failed beautifully.

to my mother and father
who taught me to navigate life's chaos by keeping your
head down when you win, and your head up when you lose.

who taught me to always remember that life
will cruelly and casually take away
everyone and everything you love,
and that even the best job with the most money
and most important sounding title will be nothing more
than cold comfort when the price you pay are hours

the silence between what i think and what i say

and days
and weeks
and years
lost with the ones you love.

this endlessly ennobling and unadorned wisdom
will provide clarity through the dark fragility
lurking just beneath the surface of american life.

so fall in love with your future if you have to:
it will provide you freedom from boredom
and the perpetuation of absolute independence.

it will be a luminous feat of generosity and humanism
among struggling souls
and faces betraying years of emotional strain.

and disregard the severe judgment of time
with its hesitancy, doubt, and uncertainty.

and look past the difficulties of self-perception
and the burden of aging.

i pray these elegies of time never fade from view,
and i pray you always have the means to see love
through these indelible, archaic pictures of beauty
that stir you in silence and hope.

i pray you have dreams painted in colors
that reality will never know,
and i pray, no matter what your age,
you never feel your life is past its most interesting parts.

for as long as you are breathing,
there is always time
to redirect,

rewind,
review,
recapture,
rediscover,
repurpose,
reconfigure,
and
redevelop
youth's redemption
by staying
exceedingly still
among the elegance of nature
and the wonders of the universe.

in between these
hushed dialogues
and shared secrets,
and through
songs of whispered reticence,

ask yourself:
what moves your spirit?
what elevates your heart?
what creates your imagination?
what makes you fully human?

is it the intimate reclamation
of what was once lost
but now found?

is it the inexhaustible restoration
and return of the integrity of our history?

is it remembering
life's precise unadmitted truth

that the greatness of men and women
is always seen in inverse proportion
to financial wealth and societal prestige?

is it looking upon
those who have direct contact
with the products of their labor,
the ones closest to nature,
the ones with dignity
and durability
and resistance?

all unyielding to the finality of life,

all knowing that luck, plain luck,
plays a big part in everything,

that grief is the final act of love,

that suffering binds you to something and someone,

that nostalgia for a life that never really existed
is still ok,

and that perhaps,
in the end,
before the final farewell,

it will be realized

that the promise of love
is not a cruel deception after all.

acknowledgements

I want to thank my publisher, the Brooklyn Writers Press and Marina Aris, who believed in my work and encouraged me to publish. Marina was one of the first to ever read these words and the first to believe this was even possible.

I want to thank my editor, Judi Heidel, whose gentle approach with thoughtful comments and suggestions made the editing process incredibly easy.

To all the others, you know who you are, and you know why I thank you. I will see you soon, and I will thank you in person.

about the author

Stephan Silich has been writing poems and short stories for over thirty years. 'The Silence Between What I Think and What I Say' is his first collection. Stephan is a native New Yorker and lives in Manhattan and East Hampton with his two daughters, Emma and Mia.

To find out more about his work and current projects, please visit:

www.brooklynwriterspress.com
www.stephansilich.com

Connect with Stephan on Instagram: @stephan_silich

Thank you for reading
The Silence Between What I Think And What I am

If you enjoyed this book, please consider leaving
a short review on Goodreads or your website of choice.

Reviews help both readers and writers.
They are an easy way to support good work and
help to encourage the continued release of quality content.

Want the latest from the Brooklyn Writers Press?
Browse our complete catalog.
www.brooklynwriterspress.com

BROOKLYN
WRITERS PRESS

www.ingramcontent.com/pod-product-compliance
Lightning Source LLC
Chambersburg PA
CBHW031111080526
44587CB00011B/932